Contents

Black Holes

Sarah Blackmore

Published in association with The Basic Skills Agency

Hodder & Stoughton

A MEMBER OF THE HODDER HEADLINE GROUP

Acknowledgements

Cover: Victor Habbick Visions/Science Photo Library

Illustrations: Sally Michel

Photos: p7 Julian Baum/Science Photo Library; p27 Mehau Kulyk/Science Photo Library

Every effort has been made to trace copyright holders of material reproduced in this book. Any rights not acknowledged will be acknowledged in subsequent printings if notice is given to the publisher.

Orders; please contact Bookpoint Ltd, 39 Milton Park, Abingdon, Oxon OX14 4TD. Telephone: (44) 01235 400414, Fax: (44) 01235 400454. Lines are open from 9.00–6.00, Monday to Saturday, with a 24 hour message answering service.
Email address: orders@bookpoint.co.uk

British Library Cataloguing in Publication Data
A catalogue record for this title is available from the British Library

ISBN 0 340 77645 5

First published 2000
Impression number   10 9 8 7 6 5 4 3 2 1
Year   2005 2004 2003 2002 2001 2000

Copyright © 1999 NTC/Contemporary Publishing Group, Inc.

Adapted for the Livewire series by Sarah Blackmore

Typeset by GreenGate Publishing Services, Tonbridge, Kent.
Printed in Great Britain for Hodder and Stoughton Educational, a division of Hodder Headline Plc, 338 Euston Road, London NW1 3BH, by Redwood Books, Trowbridge, Wilts

1 The End of a Star

Think about this.
A star that is really big.
Much, much bigger than our sun.
A giant star.

This giant star burns in its corner
of the universe.
It burns brightly for hundreds of years.
Then something very strange happens.

The star begins to die.
It comes to the end of its life.

You might think it just stops burning,
but no.
The dying star begins to fall in on itself.

All the matter that made up the star
is squeezed.
It is squeezed into a smaller
and smaller area.
Soon this giant star is no longer a giant.
It measures no more than a mile across.

The star's matter is tightly packed.
It is so tightly packed that it is very heavy.
If you could take a small piece of it.
A piece just the size of a small marble.
It would weigh as much as a mountain.

A small piece of a black hole could weigh the same amount as a mountain.

The dead star goes on falling into itself.
It pulls in every bit of matter around it.
Every speck of dust.
Every stray atom.
They are all dragged in.

This star is no longer a star.
It is a black hole.

This is what a black hole might look like. It pulls in every bit of matter around it.

2 What is a Black Hole?

What is a black hole?

Matter gets really squeezed.
Squeezed so hard that it is made
very thick and heavy.
A black hole is this area of dense matter.

It is so dense that light cannot get out.

Why is a black hole called black?

Well, no light can get out of a black hole.
So we cannot see it.
It is invisible.

How do we know that a black hole exists?

Strange things happen around a black hole.
Light that is near it just disappears.

We also know that objects in the hole
give off x-rays.
These are caused by the objects
bumping into each other.
Objects like dust particles and atoms of gas,
but we can't see these objects.
They are invisible.

3 Gravity

Just how wild is a black hole?

Well let's think about gravity.
Have you heard the saying:
'What goes up must come down'?
If you throw a ball up in the air,
it will always come back down.

Gravity pulls the ball back to Earth.
If you drop a pot
out of an upstairs window,
it will fall to the ground.
This is because gravity
pulls it to the ground.

Gravity at work.

How, then, do things pull away from Earth?

The space shuttle can pull away from Earth.
It can escape the pull of gravity.
To do this
it needs the power of giant rockets.

Now think about a planet
with more gravity than Earth.
Two or three times as much gravity.
The pull of this gravity
would be much, much stronger.

If you threw a ball up in the air
on this planet, it would still go up.
But not as far.
It would come back down much quicker.
A pot falling from an upstairs window
would fall really quickly.
This would make it really heavy.
So heavy, it could kill someone below.

On this planet, the space shuttle would need
much more powerful rockets to lift it.
More powerful than any that we use now.

There is one thing that could pull away
from this super gravity –
and that is light.

Gravity could be a million times greater
than on Earth,
and light could still get out.
In this gravity you would be crushed flat.
Flatter than your own shadow.

Now think about gravity
a billion times stronger than Earth's.
Light now has a problem.
Light trying to pull away would be bent back.

This is like the black hole.

Black hole matter is really heavy and dense.
So dense, it is hard to imagine.

Take a small piece of black hole matter.
A piece about the size of a penny.
Put it into your pocket.
It will rip through your pocket.
It will rip through the ground.
It will rip through the Earth
and come out the other side.

4 No Escape!

Have you ever spent a long time
in a waiting room?
Maybe at the dentist's or the doctor's?
Well imagine a waiting room
that you never leave.
Now you're in a black hole.
Nothing leaves.

If something goes into a black hole,
it never comes out.
It is a one-way trip.

Let's say you dropped into a black hole.
What would happen to you?
Well you would not like it.
That's for sure.

Say you went in feet first.
Your feet would be pulled down fast.
So fast that they would go much faster
than the rest of you.
You would be pulled into a thin strand
of matter.
But that's not the end.

Each atom in your body would be pulled apart.
The atoms would be pulled into smaller parts.
These are called neutrons, protons
and electrons.
This would all happen in less than a second.

Being sucked into a black hole.

5 The Fourth Dimension

A one-way trip.
Or is it?

Imagine that the trip into the black hole
did not kill you.
Some people believe
that you could move into another universe.
The fourth dimension.
At some point you would leave this universe
and enter another.
This point is called a white hole.

Moving from one universe to another!
Could a black hole be some sort
of time machine?

Mind-blowing stuff.
Is it true?

We don't know for sure.
We think there are about five black holes
just in our part of the universe.
A lot of this is guess-work.
After all nobody can see them.

One thing we do know
is that black holes do exist.
The more we find out about them,
the more they change how we think.
They change what we know about time,
space and travel.
Who knows what there is
for us to still find out.
Who knows what secrets
the black hole hides.

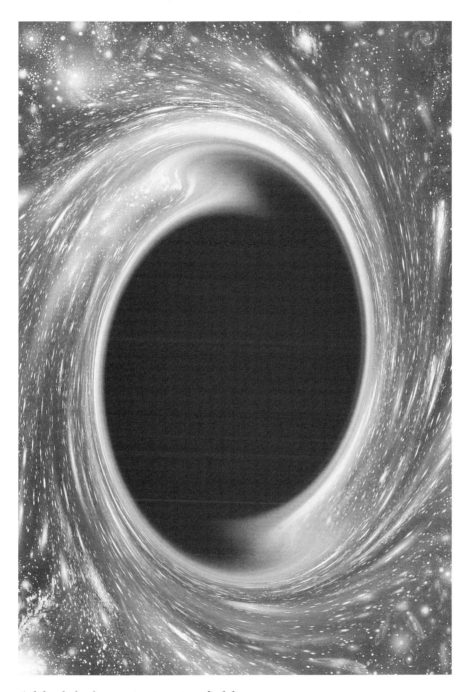

A black hole against a star-field.

Glossary of Terms Used

Atom The smallest individual part of any substance. The middle of the atom is called a nucleus. Inside the nucleus are protons and neutrons. Around the nucleus are electrons.

Electron A particle inside the atom with a negative charge.

Fourth dimension There are three dimensions in which we measure things. They are length, thickness and breadth. The fourth dimension refers to time and space.

Gravity A force of attraction. It is the force that attracts all objects towards the Earth.

Matter Matter is anything that occupies space. Matter can exist as a solid, a liquid or a gas. All matter is made up of microscopic particles such as atoms.

Neutron A particle with no charge.

Proton A particle with a positive charge.